1

YOU READ | I READ

Real Dragons!

Jennifer Szymanski

NATIONAL GEOGRAPHIC

Washington, D.C.

How to Use This Book

Reading together is fun! When older and younger readers share the experience, it opens the door to new learning. As you read together, talk about what you learn.

This side is for a parent, older sibling, or older friend. Before reading each page, take a look at the words and pictures. Talk about what you see. Point out words that might be hard for the younger reader.

This side is for the younger reader.

As you read, look for the bolded words. Talk about them before you read. In each chapter, the bolded words are:
Chapter 1: nouns • Chapter 2: action words
Chapter 3: body parts • Chapter 4: describing words

At the end of each chapter, do the activity together.

Design a dragon! Draw what you think a dragon looks like.

Table of Contents

CHAPTER 1

Are Dragons Real?

 For thousands of years, people have imagined how **dragons** might look and act if they were real. Would a dragon fly? Would it have scaly skin? Would it breathe fire?

Magical **dragons** aren't real. But many animals look like dragons. Some do things a dragon might do.

This snake looks like a dragon! It has bumpy scales that wind down its back in long rows, just like some make-believe dragons do.

It's called a dragon snake. Dragon snakes are a type of **reptile**.

 Reptiles are animals that have dry scales on their skin. Many reptiles look like dragons.

YOU READ Reptiles and make-believe dragons can have more in common than just scales. Some other parts of reptiles look like dragons, too! This Nile monitor **lizard** has long claws. It uses them to climb and dig.

READ The bearded dragon **lizard** has spikes on its neck. It puffs out its spikes when it is upset.

YOUR TURN!

Design a dragon!
Draw what you
think a dragon
looks like.

CHAPTER 2

Dragon Superpowers

YOU READ

Dragons don't have to be magical to do amazing things! The thorny dragon has a tough coat of armor. Its prickly scales **protect** it from predators. They make the thorny dragon very hard to touch or pick up.

 The thorny dragon protects itself in other ways, too. It can make its body look bigger. That may scare away a hungry animal.

The thorny dragon's super armor also makes it invisible! Its yellow and brown scales help it **blend** into the colors of its desert home. This makes the dragon hard for other animals to see.

The dragon's scales don't just **blend** in. They can change color in the sun. This helps keep the dragon cool.

This lizard can soar! The flying dragon lizard lives in some tropical rain forests. These lizards don't really fly. They use flaps made of special bones and skin to **glide** from place to place.

I READ The flying dragon **glides** between trees. It stays high in the leaves so animals on the ground can't catch it.

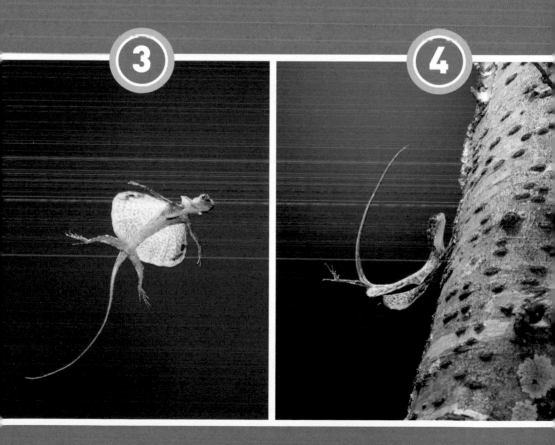

Flying dragons can also use their flaps to **scare** other animals. When the lizard is afraid, it will open its flaps, including another flap of skin on its neck. The open flaps make the lizard look larger.

 A flying dragon does not like to share its tree. If it sees another lizard, it opens its flaps of skin. This might **scare** the other lizard away.

This snake has venom powers! No animal can **spray** fire like a make-believe dragon can. But a spitting cobra comes pretty close. It can spray venom far away from its body.

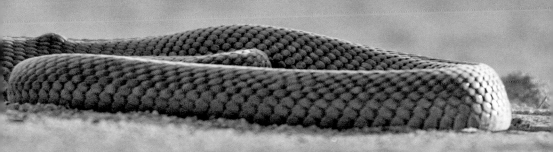

 The snake does not really spit its venom. There are small holes in the snake's fangs. The venom sprays through the holes.

YOU READ

Although the Gila (HE-lah) monster is venomous, it does not always **bite** its food. This desert lizard can open its mouth wide to swallow a yummy egg whole!

 People used to think the lizard's breath was poisonous. But its breath can't hurt an animal. It must **bite** to release its venom.

YOUR TURN!

What are these animals doing? Match the word to the picture.

1. glide
2. swallow
3. blend in
4. spray

A

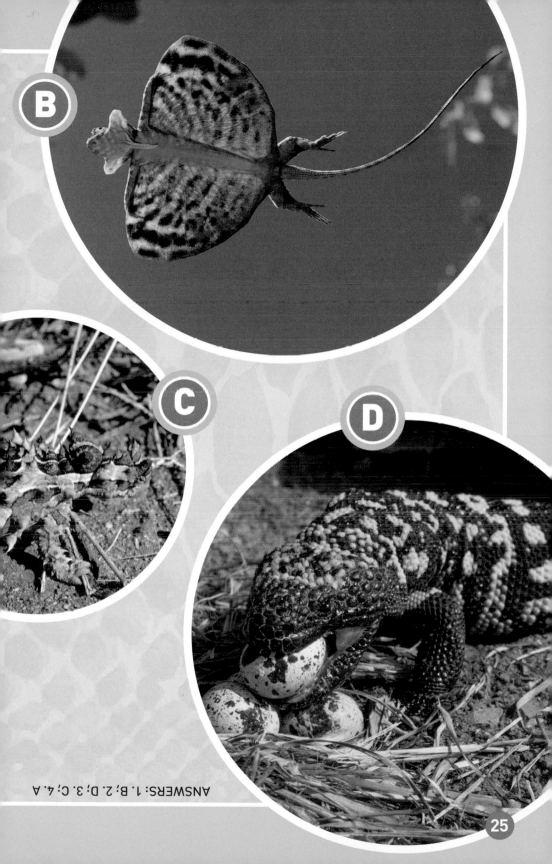

CHAPTER 3

Big Dragons

YOU READ

It might not be big enough to guard a fairy-tale castle, but the Komodo dragon is still very big. It's the biggest and heaviest living lizard on Earth. It has a powerful body, with thick, strong limbs and a long **tail**.

There is more to this dragon than its large size! It's a good runner and a good fighter. It uses its legs to run fast. It uses its **tail** to help it fight.

27

YOU READ

A Komodo dragon is a patient hunter. It hides for hours in tall grass, using its long tongue to taste the air and sense if its prey is near. When it spots a deer or water buffalo, it will use its strong body and sharp **teeth** to capture and eat it.

A dragon's mouth has many **teeth**. Each tooth is short. They are very sharp. If a tooth falls out, the dragon will grow a new one.

Its venomous bite helps the Komodo dragon finish off prey!

The Komodo dragon's **claws** are long and sharp. The dragon uses these claws to grip the ground as it runs.

 A young dragon is small. It uses its **claws** to climb a tree. It hides in the tree. Now it is safe from older dragons.

YOUR TURN!

Read each action word. Then touch the body part of the Komodo dragon that helps it do that action.

run

climb

bite

grip

CHAPTER 4

All Kinds of Dragons

 YOU READ Not all real dragons are reptiles. Fish, insects, and other kinds of animals remind people of dragons, too! The colorful dragon eel is a fish. Its mouth opens **wide**, ready to catch a meal.

 The eel has two sets of jaws. One set of jaws opens **wide** to catch food. Then the other set of jaws helps the eel swallow.

 The **bright** pink dragon millipede does not have to hide. It's not afraid of being eaten by a bird or any other animal. Its color and spines send a message to other animals.

 Its **bright** body tells other animals: Poison! Do not touch! If an animal eats it, the animal will get sick.

Does this look like a dragon? This dragonhead caterpillar has **sharp** horns on its head and tail. Its body is covered with small spikes, too. These spikes help the caterpillar defend itself.

The dragonhead caterpillar will not keep its **sharp** spikes. Soon the caterpillar will turn into a butterfly.

YOU READ Look at this animal's **long** snout! Although it looks a lot like a dragon, this fish is very gentle. It drifts and tumbles next to a coral reef.

The sea dragon is not a fast swimmer. It uses its fins and **long** tail to help steer its body through the water.

A **leafy** sea dragon's fins have
another important job, too.
The shape of its fins make
the sea dragon look a lot like
a piece of leafy seaweed.

 The sea dragon stays very still. Its **leafy** fins help it to hide in the seagrass. Other animals don't see it.

YOU READ You might have a dragon in your backyard! A dragonfly's strong wings make this insect a **fast** flier. It can dart back and forth to find food or to escape from animals that want to eat it.

Dragons can be **fast** runners or slow swimmers. Some crawl in caves. Some fly through your yard.

There are real dragons, and they are everywhere!

YOUR TURN!

Describe it! Match each word to a picture that it describes.

leafy

fast

wide

sharp

bright

long

A

For Betsy and Abby: Never stop asking questions. —J. S.

Designed by YAY! Design

The author and publisher gratefully acknowledge the expert content review of this book by Dr. Brady Barr, herpetologist and host of Nat Geo WILD's *Dangerous Encounters With Brady Barr*, and the literacy review of this book by Kimberly Gillow, principal, Milan Area Schools, Michigan.

Trade paperback ISBN: 978-1-4263-3046-9
Reinforced library binding ISBN:
978-1-4263-3047-6

Dragons in the Book
p. 1: leafy sea dragon
p. 3: giant girdled lizard
p. 5: (top) plumed basilisk; (bottom) rough-scaled bush viper
p. 6: dragon snake
p. 7: frilled lizard
p. 8: Nile monitor lizard
p. 9: bearded dragon lizard
p. 10: (top) bombardier beetle; (bottom) saltwater crocodile
p. 11: tuatara
p. 12–15: thorny dragon lizard
pp. 16–19: flying dragon lizard
p. 20: Mozambique spitting cobra
p. 21: red spitting cobra
pp. 22–23: Gila monster
p. 24: (A) Mozambique spitting cobra
p. 25: (B) horned flying lizard; (C) thorny dragon lizard; (D) Gila monster
pp. 26–33: Komodo dragon
pp. 34–35: dragon moray eel
pp. 36–37: pink dragon millipede
p. 38: dragonhead caterpillar (larva of blue nawab butterfly)
p. 39: blue nawab butterfly
pp. 40–41: weedy sea dragon
pp. 42–43: leafy sea dragon
pp. 44–45: dragonfly
p. 46: (A) green tree snake
p. 47: (C) wandering glider dragonfly; (D) Australian saltwater crocodile; (E) Chinese water dragon

Illustration Credits
GI: Getty Images; MP: Minden Pictures; SS: Shutterstock
Cover, Anna Kucherova/SS; 1, Jacqueline Lee/SS; 3, reptiles4all/SS; 4, dangdumrong/GI; 5 (UP), NNehring/GI; 5 (LO), Matthieu Berroneau; 6 (LE), reptiles4all/SS; 6 (RT), Chien Lee/MP; 7, Matt Cornish/SS; 8, Piotr Naskrecki/MP; 9 (UP), Alex Snyder; 9 (LO), Robert Valentic/MP; 10 (UP), seanjoh/GI; 10 (LO), Johnny Haglund/GI; 11 (UP), Veronika Surovtseva/SS; 11 (CTR), Kaya Dengel; 11 (LO), Pete Oxford/MP; 12-13, Marcelo_Photo/GI; 13, witte-art_de/GI; 14, Auscape/UIG/GI; 15, Alex Benwell/Alamy Stock Photo; 16-17, Satoshi Kuribayashi/MP; 18, Matthieu Berroneau; 19, Chien Lee/MP; 19 (INSET), Cyril Ruoso/Biosphoto; 20-21, Jelger Herder/MP; 21, Daniel Heuclin/Biosphoto; 22, Amwu/Dreamstime; 23, Michael D. Kern/MP; 24, Digital Vision/GI; 25 (UP), Chien Lee/MP; 25 (CTR), David South/Alamy Stock Photo; 25 (LO), Daniel Heuclin/MP; 26 (UP), Richard Susanto/SS; 26 (LO), GlobalP/GI; 27, AndreyGudkov/GI; 28, Nicolas Cegalerba/Biosphoto; 29, Sylvain Cordier/Biosphoto; 30-31, joakimbkk/GI; 31 (INSET), Andrey Gudkov/Dreamstime; 32-33, Mike Lane/MP; 34, HungryWolfProductions/GI; 35, Tony Wu; 36-37, Thailand Wildlife/Alamy Stock Photo; 38, Misterfullframe/SS; 39, Nuwat Phansuwan/SS; 40-41, WaterFrame/Alamy Stock Photo; 42 (INSET), Alex Mustard/MP; 42-43, Shin Okamoto/GI; 44, Kim Taylor/MP; 45, Fumio Nabata/AFLO/Alamy Stock Photo; 46 (LE), GraphicsRF/SS; 46 (RT), Pnwnature/Dreamstime; 47 (UP), szefei/SS; 47 (CTR LE), Steve Bower/SS; 47 (CTR RT), Andrew Burgess/SS; 47 (LO), dangdumrong/SS; heading/background (throughout), InaKos/SS

National Geographic supports K–12 educators with ELA Common Core Resources. Visit natgeoed.org/commoncore for more information.